to:
from:

Published by Sourcebooks Casablanca, an imprint of Sourcebooks, Inc.
P.O. Box 4410, Naperville, Illinois 60567-4410
(630) 961-3900
Fax: (630) 961-2168
www.sourcebooks.com

Printed and bound in the United States of America.
SP 10 9 8 7 6 5 4 3 2

love coupons

A Coupon Gift of Love and Romance

SOURCEBOOKS CASABLANCA™
AN IMPRINT OF SOURCEBOOKS, INC.®
NAPERVILLE, ILLINOIS

by Gregory J. P. Godek

the "lover's lottery" coupon

Good for three lottery tickets of your choice. If you don't win anything, the coupon-giver will create his or her own sweet reward for you.

go above and beyond

do the unexpected. give more

than you have to.

love letter

Redeem this coupon for a handwritten note from
your partner expressing his or her feelings toward you.

let your **love** inspire you at every level.

our first date redux

Redeem this coupon for a special treat: your partner will re-create the first date you shared—be it dinner or drag racing—as it was the beginning of something special.

remember the feeling you
got when you **first met?**

the random valentine coupon

Pretend it's the day of hearts and flowers on any date
except February 14th! Redeemable for the perfect romantic evening,
from dinner and drinks to chocolate hearts and favorite flowers.

romance resides

in the everyday.

dinner date

This coupon is good for one sumptuous meal prepared
by your partner, at a time of your choosing.
Don't forget to kiss the cook!

turn the ordinary
into the special.

passionate kiss coupon

Your kiss is my command! Redeem this coupon for one kiss that will make you weak in the knees...if not make you drop to the floor.

words express passion.
kissing confirms it.

massage me

This coupon entitles the holder to one tantalizing backrub,
performed by the coupon-giver.

Time limit: no less than 30 minutes in duration!

romance is a **bridge** between the sexes.

the decadent
dessert-in-bed coupon

Forget breakfast in bed—this coupon is good for luscious
treats in bed anytime of day! Start with chocolate-covered
strawberries and let your imagination run wild.

give each other
romance **every day**.

togetherness today

You are entitled to one entire day with the coupon-giver
in which you do everything together: shower, prepare meals,
do chores, make love, etc.

great relationships
aren't 50/50; they're 100/100.

the bubble bath-for-two coupon

You know what to do. Soft music, champagne, candles.

love. don't waste precious time trying to define it. spend your time **experiencing** it!

an "adventure date" coupon

Your partner will take you out somewhere neither of you have been before.

romance can happen when
you *least* expect it.

the weekend getaway coupon

Good for two days and three nights. You get to choose the weekend;
your partner chooses the location.

planning doesn't destroy
spontaneity;
it creates opportunity.

table for two

This coupon entitles you to one fancy romantic dinner with
the coupon-giver at a restaurant you choose.

smile...

you're still in love.

the "park" coupon

You are entitled to one day at a "park" of your choosing.
Options include a water park, an amusement park,
or a romantic stroll in your local neighborhood park.

the **anticipation** is often as much fun as the gift or gesture itself.

language of love

This coupon is redeemable for a day of communicating with only body language. Words prohibited. Creativity preferred.

romance is the language of love.

your wish is my command

This coupon entitles you to the fulfillment of one wish from the coupon-giver, your personal genie.

romance doesn't have to be kept under the covers.

shower of flowers

This coupon entitles you to an immediate bouquet. A dozen roses,
a bunch of wildflowers, a handful of daisies—your choice.
Flowers to be delivered within 3 days.

romance is a state of mind.
It's not so much what you do
as how you do it.

flame of love

This coupon is good for one whole night without lights.

A romantic dinner, sensual bath,

and late-night love session—all by candlelight.

it's the **meaning** that matters,

not the words.

all for you

Redeem this coupon for a session of any activity you
love but your lover doesn't. The coupon-giver vows
to enjoy the experience with you.

great relationships require
equal amounts of passion, commitment,
and intimacy.

chick flick and cuddling

This coupon is good for a night of snuggling together in front of one of your favorite romantic comedies.

become an **artist**

of your relationship.

instant picnic

Your partner brings the wine, cheese, and blanket; you bring yourself.

sometimes **romance**

just happens...

the classic, romantic, do-it-yourself coupon

_____

_____